5S

Lean Thinking Series

SUMEET SAVANT

DEDICATION

To all Lean Six Sigma enthusiasts, practitioners, and professionals.

CONTENTS

Acknowledgments xi

About the Author 1

Section I: Lean 2

Lean, value, and waste 3

House of Lean 5

Five Principles of Lean 17

Section II: Wastes 24

Types of Work 25

Need to remove wastes 30

The 3 M'S 35

Section III: Workplace Organization 40

Workplace Organization 41

Section IV: CANDO 46

CANDO by Henry Ford 47

Section V: 5S 55

5S 56

6S 60

Seiri 62

Seiton	67
Seiso	72
Seiketsu	77
Shitsuke	82
Section VI: 5S Strategies	87
5S Strategies	88
Red Tagging	89
Layout Optimization	93
Cleaning Schedule	97
Standardization	100
Sustenance for Shitsuke	104
Management Commitment	107
AUTHOR'S NOTE	108

ACKNOWLEDGMENTS

Special thanks to my wife Sahana, for always supporting me in all my endeavors and to the world of Lean Six Sigma for accepting and enabling me to perform at a global scale.

ABOUT THE AUTHOR

Sumeet Savant is a Lean Six Sigma Master Black Belt Mentor and coach, with more than a decade of experience in executing, leading and mentoring Lean Six Sigma process improvement projects. He is a BTech, MBA, and Prince certified Practitioner. He has facilitated hundreds of process improvement projects, and coached hundreds of professionals, Yellow, Green, and Black Belts over the years. He lives in Mumbai, India with his family.

LEAN

LEAN, VALUE, AND WASTE

Lean is now a common term, synonymous with process improvement, waste elimination and cost reduction.

You probably might have heard about Lean, or might have some basic idea about Lean, or might be even working on and practicing Lean methodologies

Before we start, let us understand what the term Lean really means.

Formally defined, "**Lean** is a continuous improvement strategy, focused on **maximizing customer value**, by **minimizing waste** in all the business processes, or products."

So, now the question arises, what do the terms Value and Waste mean.

"**Value**, means something, that the customer is willing to pay for, extending this definition, we can say it is something which the customer **needs, and hence expects**, from the product or service, for which he buys it.".

And, by "**Waste** we mean, any activity or feature that **does not add value** to the product or service, from the point of view of the customer."

The Japanese term for Waste so defined, is **Muda**.

Some of the examples of Waste or Muda are,

• Unnecessary travel like driving, or riding.

• Waiting for approval.

• Unnecessary Movement like bending, or stretching.

• Producing more than required.

Though Lean is primarily focused on reduction of waste, the Lean strategies framework is much broader.

To understand the Lean framework, it is a must to be well acquainted with something that is known as the **House of Lean**.

.

HOUSE OF LEAN

The collection of Lean concepts, practices, and tools, put together in a container that looks like a home, to act as a framework for implementing a complete Lean system is known as the **House of Lean.**

House of Lean: Goals

The first component of House of Lean is its roof, which represents the **Goals** of the business.

Most businesses have similar goals as follows,

• Highest Quality

Quality in terms of features and characteristics of the products or services provided to the customer.

• Lowest Cost

Lowest cost in terms of raw materials, man power, and machinery required to design, develop and deliver the products.

• **Shortest Lead Time**

Shortest time taken from initiation of idea to going to market of the products or services.

The roof of the House of quality is depicted in the following figure.

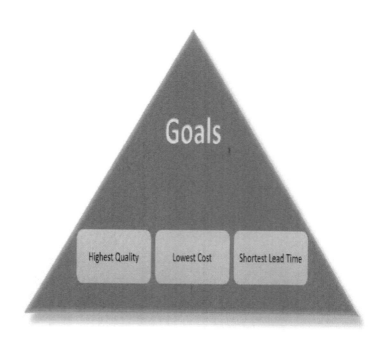

House of Lean: JIT

The next component of the House of Lean is its left pillar, which represents the **JIT or Just In Time** concepts, practices, and tools.

Just In Time

JIT is a methodology aimed primarily at reducing flow times within production system as well as response times from suppliers and to customers. It aims at reducing the inventory, and overproduction by producing just in time to meet the customer demands.

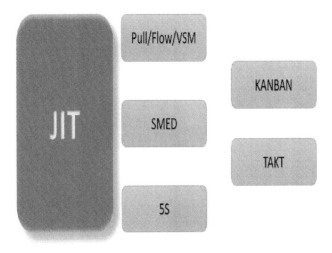

The JIT concepts, practices, and tools include the following,

• **Pull**

Pull means producing to the customer demand.

• **Flow**

In Lean, the process flow, which means to move along in a steady, continuous stream, should be free of waste, and issues, to ensure a steady continuous uninterrupted flow.

• **VSM**

Value Stream Mapping is a technique to chart the flow of the processes, identify wastes in the flow, establishing root causes for the wastes, and identifying ways to reduce or eliminate the wastes.

• **KANBAN**

Kanban is a scheduling system for lean manufacturing and just-in-time manufacturing, that makes use of cards to track, schedule and control production.

• **SMED**

Single-minute exchange of die, is a lean production method to provide a rapid and efficient way of converting a manufacturing process from running the current product to running the next product, it is a system for reducing the time taken for equipment changeovers.

• TAKT

TAKT Time, is the average time or rate at which a product needs to be completed in order to meet customer demand.

• 5S

5S is a workplace organization framework that uses five Japanese words to represent its principles or phases: Seiri(Sort), Seiton(Set in order), Seiso(Shine), Seiketsu(Standardize), and Shitsuke(Sustain).

House of Lean: JIDOKA

The next component of the House of Lean is its right pillar, which represents the **JIDOKA** concepts, practices, and tools.

JIDOKA

JIDOKA, also known as Autonomation which means "Intelligent Automation" or "Humanized Automation", is an automation which implements some sort of monitory techniques, making it "aware" enough to detect an abnormal situation, and stop the machine, to enable the workers to stop the production line, investigate the root causes and fix the issue.

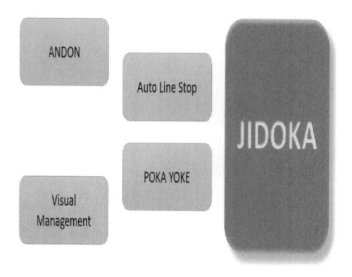

The JIDOKA concepts, practices, and tools include the following,

• ANDON

ANDON is an alerting system that notifies management, maintenance, and other workers of a quality or process problem. It can be manual or automated.

• Auto Line Stop

Auto Line Stop is a system that stops the production process whenever an issue or defect occurs, it can be automated or manual.

• POKA YOKE

POKA YOKE or Mistake Proofing, is a lean mechanism that helps an equipment operator avoid (yokeru) mistakes (poka). It eliminates product defects by preventing, correcting, or drawing attention to human errors as they occur.

• Visual Management

Visual Management is a lean system to manage production and processes through visual signs and controls.

House of Lean: Standardization and Stability

The next component of the House of Lean is its strong base, which represents the **Standardization and Stability** concepts, practices, and tools.

Standardization and Stability

Standardization and Stability, deal with standardizing the work, processes, and workplace, with an aim to consistently achieve the best, and with stabilizing the processes to avoid fluctuations and variations in output.

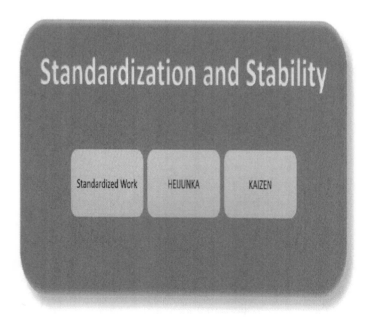

The Standardization and Stability concepts, practices, and

tools include the following,

• Standardized Work

Standardized Work is a work derived from best practices and lessons learned while performing the work, to do it in a most efficient way, to improve productivity and avoid rework.

• HEIJUNKA

HEIJUNKA or leveling, is a technique to level the work or production load to reduce unevenness or Mura.

• KAIZEN

KAIZEN is a continuous improvement approach based on the idea that small, continuous or consistent positive changes can reap major improvements.

House of Lean: Respect for Individual

The final and core component of the House of Lean is to establish the values of **Respect for Individual**.

Respect for Individual

Respect for Individual, deals with empowering, motivating, and supporting the workforce to effectively and consistently participate in lean methodologies to guarantee and sustain improvements.

The Respect for Individual concepts, practices, and tools include the following,

• Empowerment, Motivation, and Support

Empowerment, Motivation, and Support is a management philosophy and ideology to empower, motivate, and support the workforce to encourage them identify the areas for improvement, and participate consistently and willingly without the need to be told to do so.

• Gemba Kaizen Circles

Gemba Kaizen is a Japanese concept of continuous improvement designed for enhancing processes and reducing waste at the workplace including the workforce, or the people that work at the location. Gemba refers to the location where value is created, while Kaizen relates to improvements.

• HOSHIN Planning

HOSHIN Planning is a strategic planning process in which strategic goals are communicated throughout the company and then put into action.

House of Lean

With all the components combined, the House of Lean looks similar to the following depicted figure.

FIVE PRINCIPLES OF LEAN

There are five principles of lean, based around customer, values, quality and wastes. They are,

Define Value

To be able to understand the first principle of Lean, it is essential to know what "Value" and "Quality" are.

Value is something that the customer is willing to pay for. It is something that the customer expects from the product or service, he buys. It is something, which satisfies the customer's needs.

Quality of a product or service is the degree of value the product or service adds to the customer. It means, the degree to which the product or service satisfies the customer's needs

For a company to survive and succeed, it is essential that it understands the needs of its customers, and how its products and services can satisfy its customer's needs by providing the right quality and adding the right value.

So, it is very essential to identify and define value from the point of view of the customer, and produce products and services that deliver maximum quality, and value.

Due to this reason, the very first principle in lean states to define or identify value from the point of view of the customer.

What is valuable to customer, or what are the customer's needs can be found out by collecting the VOC or the **Voice of customer**.

There are many ways VOC can be gathered, such as interviews, surveys, and market and web analytics that can help you discover what customers seek value in.

Map Value Stream

Once you identify what the customer values in your products or services, the next step is to understand the steps and activities involved in creating the value.

The **Value stream** is the complete end to end flow of a product's life-cycle.

It starts from the getting the raw materials used to make the product, and goes on up to the customer's buying, using, and ultimately disposing of the product.

Mapping the Value Stream, in this context, is an exercise to create a flowchart or a process map of all the activities involved in the product's complete life cycle.

The **Value stream process map** thus created outlines each and every step of the process for each part of the business, right from market research, to R&D, to Design, to Development, to Production, to Marketing, to Sales and Services, etc.

Only by thoroughly studying and understanding the value stream can a company understand the wastes associated, and hence find opportunities to reduce costs and tackle issues, in manufacturing and delivery of a product or service.

Supplier and customer partnership is one of the core ideas of Lean as it helps understand the complete supply chain, and eliminate wastes and other issues from the entire value stream.

Create Flow

Once you have the Value Stream Map ready, the next step will be to create Flow.

To **Create Flow**, means to ensure that the flow of the process steps is smooth and free of interruptions or delays.

The first action to achieve this is to analyze the process map for wastes.

Once the wastes are analyzed, you can perform root cause analysis to understand the causes behind the wastes.

These causes needs to be acted upon to ensure the flow of steps and activities are smoothed and made free of any issues, problems, or bottlenecks.

Once the wastes are eliminated, you can find further ways to maximize efficiencies.

Some strategies for ensuring smooth flow include breaking down steps, re-engineering the steps, work and production leveling, creating cross-functional and multi-skilled departments, suppliers, and workforce.

Establish Pull

Once you have eliminated the wastes in the process, and created the flow, the next step would be to establish Pull.

Pull is producing as per customer demand.

Inventory and Overproduction are two of the most problematic wastes in any production systems.

The ultimate goal of the pull system is to limit stocking up the inventory, and to produce only to meet the customer demand

To achieve this, you need to effectively look at the operations of the business in reverse on the value stream maps.

The idea is to capture and analyze the exact moments as to when the customers actually need the product.

This helps to implement the JIT mode of manufacturing and operations where products are produced just in time when the customers need them.

Extending this further, this also helps to get and procure even the raw materials, just in time when the production needs them.

Pursue Perfection

Once you have eliminated the wastes in the process, created the flow, and established the Pull, the final step is to keep the improvements sustained, and ongoing.

Perfection is to achieve the absolute best in anything that the company does.

So, it is absolutely not enough to just eliminate wastes, create flow, and establish pull.

You need to develop a mindset of continual improvement.

Each and every employee should strive towards perfection, and work with an aim to deliver consistent value.

This relentless pursuit of perfection is key attitude of an organization that is "going for lean", and makes Lean thinking and continuous process improvement a part of the organizational culture.

The following figure depicts the five principles of Lean.

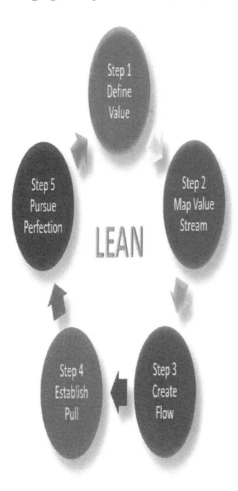

WASTES

TYPES OF WORK

Before we can understand what waste is, it is very important to understand what are the types of work.

There are three types of work based on the customer's point of view, as to how the customer looks at the work done.

They are,

- **Value Added Work**

- **Business Necessary Work**

- **Non Value Added Work**

Now, we will see each of these work types in detail.

Value Added Work

Value Added Work is the first type of work activity.

It is type of activity or work, for which the customer is willing to pay for.

Any activity which the customer perceives as actually adding value to the product or service is termed as **Value Added Work**.

These activities have the following characteristics which classify these activities as value adding.

• **Change/Transformation**

These activities change or transform an item from one condition to another, or from one state to another, with an overall focus of reaching the final state of the product or service, which the customer needs.

• **First Time Right**

These activities are done in a right way, or correctly the very first time, that is without the need for corrections or rework.

• **Customer is willing to pay**

These activities are activities which the customer wants done, as he perceives them to be necessary steps to create the product or service he expects, and hence is willing to pay for.

Business Necessary Work

Business Necessary Work is the second type of work activity.

It is type of activity or work, for which though the customer is unwilling to pay, still needs to be performed to create the product or services the customer needs.

This type of activity may have similar characteristics as Value Adding Activity like, transformation of an item from one state to another, or done correctly the first time.

However, the important difference which classify this type of activity differently is that the customer does not care for this activity, and hence is unwilling to pay.

Such work includes any work that might be performed to protect the business, or to comply with established policies or standards, or even as precautionary measures.

This type of work is also known as the following,

• **Business Value Added Work.**

• **Value Enabling Work.**

• **Necessary Non Value Added Work.**

Non Value Added Work

Non Value Added Work is the third type of work activity.

This work activity adds absolutely no value to the product or service.

This work activity neither transforms nor helps in achieving the end product or service.

And most importantly, the customer is not willing to pay for this work activity.

This work activity is referred to as waste, or the **Muda** in Japanese.

To figure out any non value activity in your products or service, it is best to look at them from the point of view of customer, and think whether the customer would be willing to pay for the activity.

Lean focuses on eliminating waste, by reducing or removing the non value activities from the value stream.

Example

Imagine you need to travel from one city to another, on a road.

Traveling on the road represents the value flow, as it helps you reach your destination.

Value added work would be you driving a vehicle on that road to reach your destination.

Non Value added work would be any additional turns, stops, and interruptions you may have to take while driving due to various reasons like traffic, broken pathways, pedestrians crossing roads etc.

Business Value added work would be any additional turns, stops interruptions you may have to take while driving due to the road and traffic rules like the zebra crossing, traffic lights, etc.

.

NEED TO REMOVE WASTES

Before we proceed any further, let us quickly look at a visual representation that will help you understand how important it is to remove waste from our services and products.

Consider a process, a typical process will have certain value added activities, and certain non value added activities.

Following is a depiction of a value stream of such a typical process.

Value added work is depicted in green, and non value added work in red.

This may appear quite normal, and acceptable, however just wait and watch, what happens when we analyze it.

Looking at the value stream map, we may think that it depicted a normal acceptable waste presence.

However, let us now split, and separate the value added work from the non value added work.

Now look at the newly arranged value stream map, depicted in the following figure.

You will get to clearly see what the wastes are doing to our processes.

As you can see, the minor wastes hidden here and there when taken together do appear huge, and sometimes huge enough to harm the process.

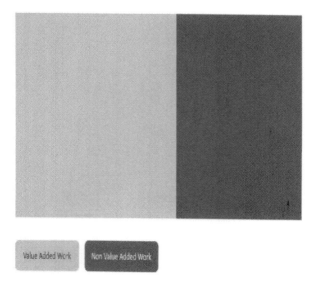

Value Added Work   Non Value Added Work

Let us continue the analysis one more step further.

Let us now actually calculate the percentage distribution of the value added and the non value added work or activity in our process.

And then let us plot the distribution in a pie chart, to get a visual feel of the percentage distribution.

Depicted below is the figure of pie distribution so created.

If you see, the total waste in our process is 43%, with so much waste hidden in our processes no wonder they are so costly.

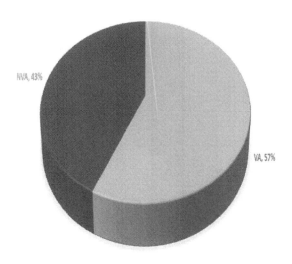

PERCENTAGE DISTRIBUTION

Lean focuses on saving these costs, by eliminating wastes and improving processes.

Imagine that the total time taken by our process is 2000 person hours, and per hour uniform cost of 50 USD.

So, the total cost of our process then would be 100000 USD

And, since 43% of the time was going waste,

The process clearly wasted as much as 860 person hour per run, and a dollar wastage of 43000 USD

If we now consider that this process runs just even once per day, just imagine the kind of loss this process is creating annually.

The reason why Lean is so powerful is that it focuses on searching such opportunities where costs can be saved.

And, as we have seen so far, to achieve the highest cost reductions in our processes, it is imperative that we need to hunt for wastes in them.

And, to hunt for wastes, we need to have a clear understanding of what the wastes are, their types, and how we can control and eliminate them.

THE 3 M'S

Any discussion on wastes, will be incomplete if we do not talk about the 3 infamous M's in the Lean world, the Muda, Muri, and Mura.

Muda

Muda in Japanese means useless, or waste, and comes in eight forms.

The figure below clearly depicts Muda, as can be seen, the truck is not being utilized to its fullest capacity, and hence considerable space is being **wasted**.

Muri

Muri is the overloading or overburdening of employees, or machines, or processes.

Employees, machines, and even processes, have thresholds or limits, which should be respected.

Trying to get more done from them, beyond their capacity, can lead to break downs or stress, and low morale.

The figure below clearly depicts Muri, as can be seen, the truck is overloaded to the point of tipping or loosing balance.

Establishing TAKT time, standardizing work, and implementing pull systems are some of the ways to avoid Muri.

OVERLOAD

Mura

Mura is the unevenness or fluctuation or variation in the work, or workplace.

We often see this in products and services due to rushed delivery, or poor planning.

Establishing TAKT time, leveling work (Heijunka), implementing Six Sigma and pull systems are some of the ways to avoid Mura.

The figure below clearly depicts Mura, as can be seen, the two carriages of the truck are unevenly loaded.

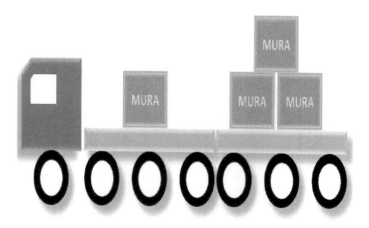

UNEVENNESS

The Ideal State

No Muda, No Muri, and No Mura is the ideal state to be achieved and sustained in any lean system.

Processes should be free or wastes, overloading, and unevenness or variation.

The figure below clearly depicts a No Muda, Muri, Mura state, as can be seen, the truck is carrying just the ideal load, free of the 3 M's.

NO MUDA, NO MURI, NO MURA

WORKPLACE ORGANIZATION

WORKPLACE ORGANIZATION

Before we get into an in depth understanding of the 5S methodology, it is essential we first take a look at what the following related terms mean,

• **Work**.

• **Workplace**.

• **Workplace productivity**.

• **Workplace organization**.

Work

Work in simple terms is an action taken to accomplish something meaningful for the person or a group of people performing the action.

Work has different meanings in different contexts like it can be a work of art, a work of music, a work in religion, a work in physics, a work in literature, a work as in employment, or even a work that happens in business.

Work in context of the 5S, can mean two related things.

It can be,

• Work that the employed workforce of businesses do to earn a livelihood.

• Work that the businesses get done from the workforce in order to create products or services for their customers.

Workplace

Workplace as we know, in simple terms is a place, or a location, where the work happens.

It can be a factory assembly floor, or a offshore dedicated center, or even a home for home run businesses.

And, from lean management point of view **Workplace** is a place where the businesses focus on developing quality products with maximum value.

It is interesting to note that on an average any working personal spends at least 40% of his daily time at a work place.

Workplace productivity

Workplace productivity is the direct measurement of how productive the workplace is.

Businesses spend high amount of money on the workforce to create quality products, and higher the productivity, greater is the benefit to the businesses.

Productivity at workplace can take serious hit if the people waste their time and effort doing non value adding activities.

Some of the non value adding activities that the workforce can waste doing are,

• Searching for tools and materials.

• Walking distances to fetch the required tools and materials.

• Stretching, bending, and twisting to reach necessary tools and materials.

All this is a direct result of poor workplace organization.

Workplace Organization

Workplace Organization is a strategy to organize the workplace in order to make it most effective.

It focuses on increasing the overall productivity it can derive from the workforce working at the workplace.

And reduce the overall non value adding activities the workforce spend their valuable time and effort on.

Workplace organization directly benefits the businesses by increasing the overall productivity, and hence reducing the wastes and hence costs.

At the same time, it also benefits the workforce by making the work simple, pleasurable and comfortable.

CANDO

CANDO BY HENRY FORD

Having understood what work, workplace, workplace productivity, and workplace organization mean, there is just one more thing to understand before we can proceed with the 5S system.

That is to understand the method from which the 5S system is believed to have been inspired, the CANDO.

Henry Ford, from America, the founder of the Ford Motor Company was the pioneer who sponsored the development of the assembly line technique of mass production, and the founder of Mass Production.

CANDO was a method developed by Ford, to create clean, and orderly workplace that exposed waste, and increased the efficiency of all processes involved in the manufacturing unit.

It was this efficient workplace management system that inspired the Toyota leaders, to invent the 5S method..

The following figure depicts the CANDO methodology.

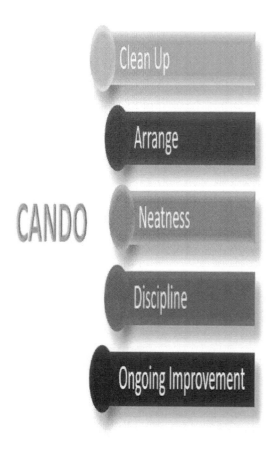

Clean Up

Clean Up focused on keeping the workplace clean of wastes, unused, and unnecessary things like used up raw materials, oil, grease, nuts, bolts, tools, dirt, dust, scraps, garbage among others.

It was achieved by keeping the factory floor, the assembly line, the tools, the engines, the machines, and the work stations clean post use.

It promoted safety, productivity, and efficiency by helping to notice parts and pieces which needed to be repaired, or replaced, ensuring continued production, and boosting morale of the employee..

Arrange

Arrange focused on labeling and arranging in order all workplace instruments like nuts, bolts, cutters, saws, pins, screw drivers, knives, pin punches, pin vises, jaws, pliers, files, wrenches, strippers, pullers, scrapers, reamers among others.

It was achieved by labeling the instruments and tools, identifying their ascending or descending orders and keeping them in the right place, as per the order decided.

It promoted visual workplace, visual control, and productivity by reducing the time to search for instruments drastically and minimizing the frustration of the employee, and hence boosting their morale, and enthusiasm..

Neat

Neat focused on keeping the workplace neat by identifying useful instruments and tools and discarding any instruments that were no longer useful.

It was achieved by identifying the different instruments and tools present on the workplace, understanding why each item is used, where it is used, when and how much it is used, and discarding all items which are no longer useful.

It promoted effective utilization of space, helped keep the workplace tidy, reduce the time to hunt for instruments drastically, and hence minimized the frustration of the employee, and boosted their morale, and enthusiasm..

Discipline

Discipline focused on keeping the workplace and the first three principles disciplined by identifying effective means and ways to ensure the CANDO principles are performed, and followed in a disciplined way.

It was achieved by identifying and setting clear standards, clear policies, and simple procedures, and rules.

It promoted disciplined participation and hence improvements by setting up a formal processes to evaluate effectiveness, and providing the necessary frameworks and policies within which to achieve the benefits of CANDO.

.

Ongoing Improvement

Ongoing Improvement focused on ensuring ongoing and sustained improvements by identifying effective means and ways to ensure the CANDO principles are strictly adhered to.

It was achieved by identifying and setting up review mechanisms, audit mechanisms, reward and award mechanisms, and providing training as and when needed.

It promoted continued participation and sustained ongoing improvements by setting up a formal processes to evaluate effectiveness, frameworks within which to review and audit compliance and adherence, and means for regular inspections, recognition and feedback.

The following figure depicts the detailed CANDO methodology.

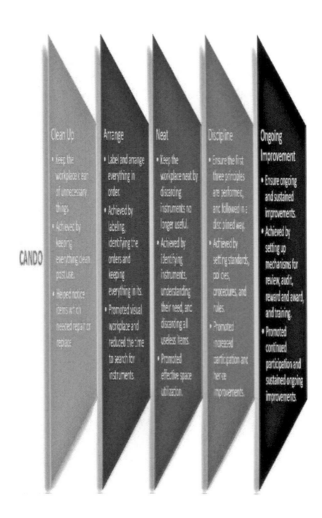

5 S

5S

Having understood **CANDO** the method from which the 5S system is believed to have been inspired, it is a good time now to have a quick overview of the 5S system.

5S, is a workplace organization system that makes use of the following five Japanese words.

Seiri is sorting through of items in a workplace and discarding all unnecessary ones.

Seiton is setting the left necessary items in an optimal order for fulfilling their function in the workplace.

Seiso is shining, cleaning and inspecting the workplace, for tools and machinery on a regular basis.

Seiketsu is standardizing the processes used to sorting, setting in order and shining the workplace.

Shitsuke is sustaining the developed processes by self-discipline of the workers.

Inspired by this efficient workplace management system, the west renamed the Japanese 5 S system with 5 English words as Sort, Set in Order, Shine, Standardize, and Sustain.

The following figure depicts the Japanese 5S
methodology.

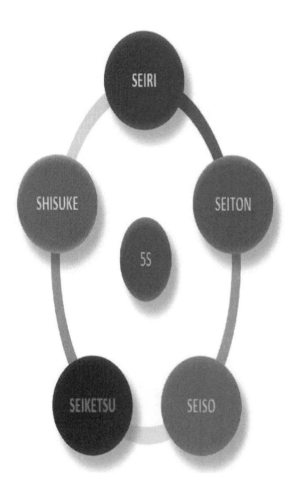

The following figure depicts the English adapted 5S methodology.

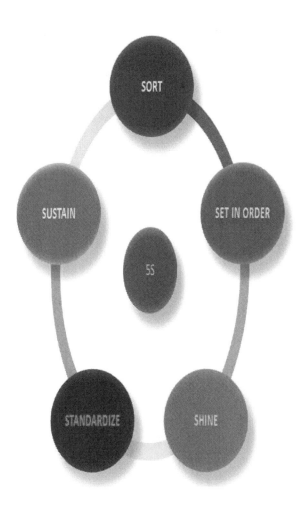

6S

Having got a brief idea of the 5S system, it is a good time to understand the 6th S.

6S, often times known as 5S + Safety is a system that adheres to the 5S principle of Sort, Set in order, Shine, Standardize, and Sustain, and also adds the concept of Safety.

So, 6S, not only helps organizations promote efficient working environments but also establishes a sustainable culture of safety.

Safety is identifying hazards and setting preventive controls to keep workers safe during work operations.

Though the intention of promoting safety is relevant, however, most followers of the original 5S system, and the Lean insist that there is no need for an additional S, as the

5 S anyway achieves safety requirements by default, and that safety is the minimum hygiene factor.

SEIRI

Now we will see each of the 5 S in order, and understand its purpose, what it means, how it can be achieved, and why it is necessary. Starting with the first S, i.e. Seiri.

Purpose, the purpose of Seiri is to keep the workplace free of waste.

English Meaning(s), the English meanings or synonyms to the Japanese word Seiri are Organize, Arrangement, Sorting, Adjustment, Regulation.

Equivalent in English 5S system, The equivalent word in the English 5S system is Sort.

Seiri: What it means

Seiri is the first principle or phase or activity of the 5S system or methodology and focuses on ensuring things are kept sorted.

It involves checking all the items in the location and sorting them in terms of their usage.

The workplace is then freed from all unnecessary items by eliminating or removing or discarding them..

Seiri: How it can be achieved

To perform Seiri in the workplace,

• List out all the items in the workplace.

• Decide which items you need.

• Sort them in terms of usage, need, and frequency of use.

• Distinguish necessary and unnecessary.

• Discard all unwanted, unused, damaged, or broken items..

Seiri: Why is it necessary

Performing Seiri is essential as,

• It helps remove scrap, and in waste reduction.

• It helps reduce time and effort spent in finding items, by reducing the number of items.

• It helps in effective space utilization.

• It helps making the workplace safer by removing damaged and faulty parts or items.

• It helps reduce the probability of distraction by removing unwanted items.

• It ensures productivity, effective available space utilization and workforce safety.

The following figure depicts the first S, i.e. Seiri.

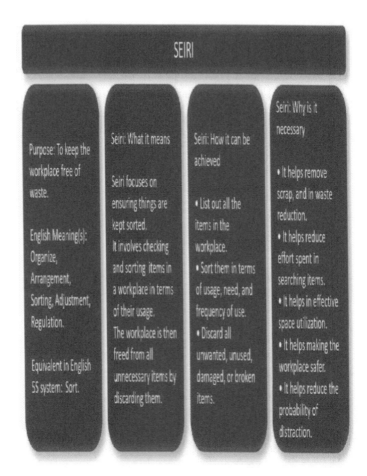

SEIRI

Purpose: To keep the workplace free of waste.

English Meaning(s): Organize, Arrangement, Sorting, Adjustment, Regulation.

Equivalent in English 5S system: Sort.

Seiri: What it means

Seiri focuses on ensuring things are kept sorted. It involves checking and sorting items in a workplace in terms of their usage. The workplace is then freed from all unnecessary items by discarding them.

Seiri: How it can be achieved

• List out all the items in the workplace.
• Sort them in terms of usage, need, and frequency of use.
• Discard all unwanted, unused, damaged, or broken items.

Seiri: Why is it necessary

• It helps remove scrap, and in waste reduction.
• It helps reduce effort spent in searching items.
• It helps in effective space utilization.
• It helps making the workplace safer.
• It helps reduce the probability of distraction.

SEITON

Now that we got a good understanding of Seiri, we will now look at the next S, i.e. Seiton.

Purpose, the purpose of Seiton is to keep the workplace appropriately ordered.

English Meaning(s), the English meanings or synonyms to the Japanese word Seiton are Tidy, Orderliness, Arranging neatly.

Equivalent in English 5S system, The equivalent word in the English 5S system is Set in Order.

Seiton: What it means

Seiton is the second principle or phase or activity of the 5S system or methodology and focuses on ensuring things are kept ordered.

It involves checking all the items in the location and arranging them in an optimal way for fulfilling their function.

The workplace is then tidied as all the items are set in order.

Seiton: How it can be achieved

To perform Seiton in the workplace,

• Arrange work stations in close proximity of all tools and equipment.

• As an alternate, get all the tools or equipment near work stations for easy and quick retrieval.

• Set them in order, as per their uses, with the most frequently used items nearest to the workplace.

• Set them in order so that they can be easily selected for use.

• Assign fixed locations for items.

• Label the locations fixed for the items.

Seiton: Why is it necessary

Performing Seiton is essential as,

• It helps arrange equipment and items in a logical order.

• It helps in easy retrieval of items by making them easy to reach, and easy to spot.

• It helps to make the tools and items easy to select for the right purpose.

• It helps reduce the time and effort spent in searching for the right tool for purpose from a bunch of irrelevant ones.

• It helps to spot missing items, as any missing of items from an ordered set is much easy to detect.

• It helps implement visual control, by implementing visual labeled locations.

The following figure depicts the second S, i.e. Seiton.

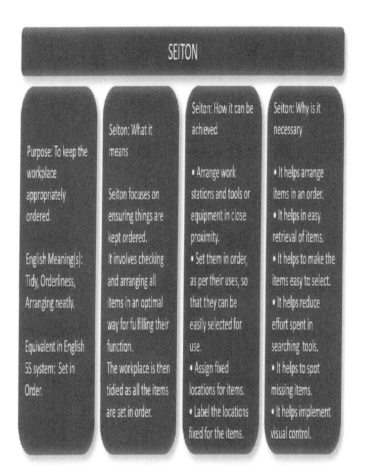

SEITON

Purpose: To keep the workplace appropriately ordered.

English Meaning(s): Tidy, Orderliness, Arranging neatly.

Equivalent in English 5S system: Set in Order.

Seiton: What it means

Seiton focuses on ensuring things are kept ordered. It involves checking and arranging all items in an optimal way for fulfilling their function. The workplace is then tidied as all the items are set in order.

Seiton: How it can be achieved

• Arrange work stations and tools or equipment in close proximity.
• Set them in order, as per their uses, so that they can be easily selected for use.
• Assign fixed locations for items.
• Label the locations fixed for the items.

Seiton: Why is it necessary

• It helps arrange items in an order.
• It helps in easy retrieval of items.
• It helps to make the items easy to select.
• It helps reduce effort spent in searching tools.
• It helps to spot missing items.
• It helps implement visual control.

SEISO

Now that we got a good understanding of Seiri, and Seiton, we will now look at the next S, i.e. Seiso.

Purpose, the purpose of Seiso is to keep the workplace clean.

English Meaning(s), the English meanings or synonyms to the Japanese word Seiso is Neat.

Equivalent in English 5S system, The equivalent word in the English 5S system is Shine. their process improvement ideas.

Seiso: What it means

Seiso is the third principle or phase or activity of the 5S system or methodology and focuses on ensuring the workplace and things in it are kept clean.

It involves sweeping, cleaning, and inspecting the entire workplace, and all the tools, equipment, machinery, and everything else in the it and keeping everything neat.

The workplace is freed from dirt, dust, oil, scrap, filth, and all other kinds of waste, to the point that it literally shines.

Seiso: How it can be achieved

To perform Seiso in the workplace,

• Keep all the work stations clean.

• Keep all the tools, equipment, machinery clean.

• Set up a scheduled frequency to perform cleaning activity, preferably daily.

• Inspect the workstations, the workplace, and all equipment while cleaning.

Seiso: Why is it necessary

Performing Seiso is essential as,

• It helps keep the workplace clean, and hence pleasing to work in.

• It helps keep the workplace safe.

• It helps to take prompt action on equipment that needs repair or replacement, hence it helps in continued production.

• It helps easy and early detection of issues, and problems.

The following figure depicts the third S, i.e. Seiso.

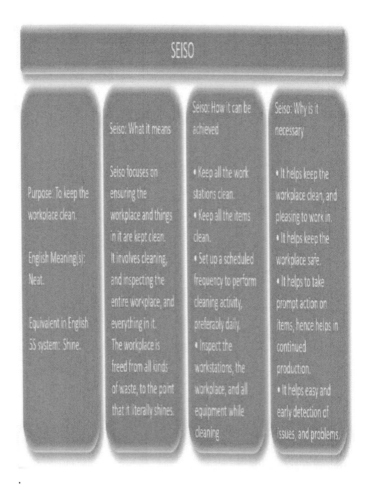

SEISO

Purpose: To keep the workplace clean.

English Meaning(s): Neat.

Equivalent in English 5S system: Shine.

Seiso: What it means

Seiso focuses on ensuring the workplace and things in it are kept clean. It involves cleaning, and inspecting the entire workplace, and everything in it. The workplace is freed from all kinds of waste, to the point that it literally shines.

Seiso: How it can be achieved

• Keep all the work stations clean.
• Keep all the items clean.
• Set up a scheduled frequency to perform cleaning activity, preferably daily.
• Inspect the workstations, the workplace, and all equipment while cleaning

Seiso: Why is it necessary

• It helps keep the workplace clean, and pleasing to work in.
• It helps keep the workplace safe.
• It helps to take prompt action on items, hence helps in continued production.
• It helps easy and early detection of issues, and problems.

SEIKETSU

Now that we got a good understanding of Seiri, Seiton, and Seiso we will now look at the next S, i.e. Seiketsu.

Purpose, the purpose of Seiketsu is to standardize the processes to perform the first 3S in the workplace.

English Meaning(s), the English meanings or synonyms to the Japanese word Seiketsu are Cleanliness, Cleansed, Neat, Unpolluted, Scrubbed, Unsoiled, Stainless, Unstained, Washed.

Equivalent in English 5S system, The equivalent word in the English 5S system is Standardize.

Seiketsu: What it means

Seiketsu is the fourth principle or phase or activity of the 5S system or methodology and focuses on ensuring proper processes, and schedules are in place to perform the first 3S in the workplace.

It involves standardizing the methods and measures to perform and evaluate the 3S in workplace.

The workforce is provided with guidelines, with which it can keep the workplace free of waste, ordered, and clean.

Seiketsu: How it can be achieved

To perform Seiketsu in the workplace,

• Make the first 3S a part of daily routine.

• Develop processes, practices, policies, guidelines, standards to perform the first 3S.

• Communicate the responsibilities to each employee to keep the workplace clean, sorted, and ordered.

• Inspect that the operations are being followed by the workforce as per mentioned, and help when needed.

Seiketsu: Why is it necessary

Performing Seiketsu is essential as,

• It helps to establish easy to perform steps to keep the workplace sorted, ordered and clean.

• It helps to make everyone understand their responsibilities to keep their workplace organized.

• It promotes participation.

The following figure depicts the fourth S, i.e. Seiketsu.

SEIKETSU

| Purpose: To standardize the processes to perform the first 3S in the workplace.

English Meaning(s): Cleanliness, Cleansed, Neat, Unpolluted, Scrubbed, Unsoiled, Stainless, Washed.

Equivalent in English 5S system: Standardize. |

| Seiketsu: What it means

Seiketsu focuses on ensuring proper processes are in place to perform the 3S. It involves standardizing 3S methods and measures. It provides guidelines, to keep the workplace free of waste, ordered, and clean. |

| Seiketsu: How it can be achieved

• Make the first 3S a part of daily routine.
• Develop processes, practices, policies to perform the first 3S.
• Communicate the responsibilities to keep workplace clean, sorted, and ordered.
• Inspect the operations and help when needed. |

| Seiketsu: Why is it necessary

• It helps to establish easy to perform steps to keep the workplace sorted, ordered and clean.
• It helps to make everyone understand their responsibilities to keep their workplace organized.
• It promotes participation. |

SHITSUKE

Now that we got a good understanding of Seiri, Seiton, Seiso and Seiketsu we will now look at the next and the final S, i.e. Shitsuke.

Purpose, the purpose of Shitsuke is to ensure ongoing and sustained 3S improvements in the workplace.

English Meaning(s), the English meanings or synonyms to the Japanese word Shitsuke are Discipline.

Equivalent in English 5S system, The equivalent word in the English 5S system is Sustain. management can establish themselves as role models can the workforce be inspired and participate.

Shitsuke: What it means

Shitsuke is the fifth principle or phase or activity of the 5S system or methodology and focuses on ensuring that the processes implemented to perform the first 3S in the workplace, are indeed being followed regularly.

It involves disciplining the workforce to keep up the focus and rigor in the 3S in workplace, to keep the accomplishments sustained.

The workforce is disciplined positively, empowering it to instill a sense of self-discipline with which it can keep the workplace free of waste, ordered, and clean, without being told.

Shitsuke: How it can be achieved

To perform Shitsuke in the workplace,

• Maintain the established standards and review them periodically.

• Conduct training to encourage the workforce.

• Conduct audits to ensure the standards maintained are followed by the workforce.

• Identify ways to improve things continually.

• Take feedback from the workforce to make processes better and easy.

• Take care of any issues promptly, figure out the root causes and fix them and prevent them from recurring.

Shitsuke: Why is it necessary

Performing Shitsuke is essential as,

• It helps to sustain the accomplishments already achieved.

• It helps to keep up the focus on continuous improvement of the workplace.

• It helps to promote and ensure continued participation from the workforce.

• It helps to ensure that the 5S approach is followed and sustained.

The following figure depicts the fifth S, i.e. Shitsuke.

SHITSUKE			
Purpose: To ensure ongoing and sustained 3S improvements in the workplace. English Meaning(s): Discipline. Equivalent in English 5S system: Sustain.	Shitsuke: What it means Shitsuke focuses on ensuring the 3S processes are followed regularly. It involves disciplining the workforce to keep the 3S results and achievements sustained. It positively disciplines by letting workforce to perform without being told.	Shitsuke: How it can be achieved • Maintain and review standards. • Conduct training to encourage workforce. • Conduct audits to ensure the standards are followed. • Identify ways to improve continually, by taking feedback from the workforce. • Take care of issues promptly.	Shitsuke: Why is it necessary • It helps to sustain the accomplishments already achieved. • It helps keep up the focus on continuous improvement in the workplace. • It helps ensure continued workforce participation. • It helps ensure 5S approach is followed and sustained.

.

5S STRATEGIES

5S STRATEGIES

Now that we got a good understanding of the 5S system, it is a good time to have a look at some of the best strategies to implement the 5S.

We will be looking at the following 5S strategies,

Red Tagging.

Layout Optimization.

Cleaning Schedule.

Standardization.

Sustenance..

RED TAGGING

Red Tagging is the most effective strategy to keep the workplace free of waste, and hence it helps achieve Seiri in the workplace.

It is used to check all the items in the workplace, and identify and **Red Tag** the unnecessary items.

Red Tags, are tags that capture the information of the identified unnecessary items like the Item Name, the reason for marking it unnecessary, the decision date, the approval and authorization details for disposal, and the disposal date.

The following figure depicts a sample Red Tag, note that the details captured can be customized as needed.

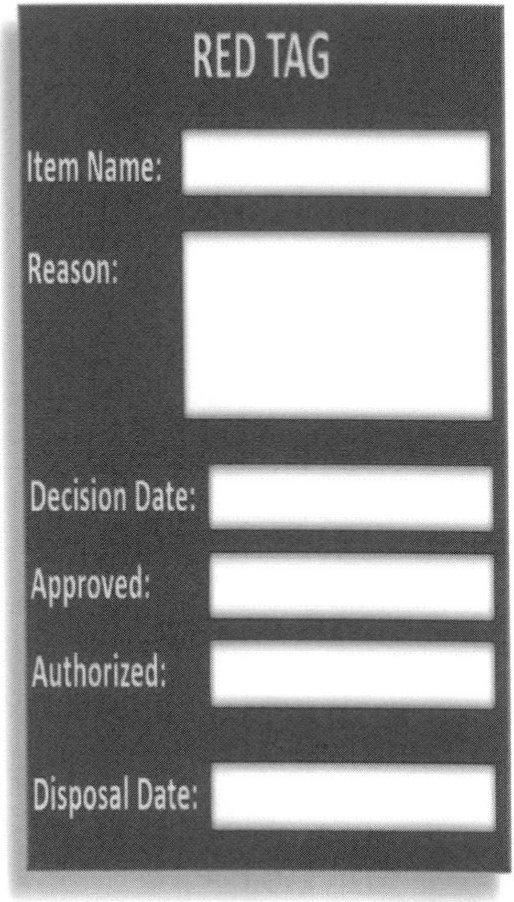

RED TAG

Item Name:

Reason:

Decision Date:

Approved:

Authorized:

Disposal Date:

Red Tagging: Process

Red Tagging often times involve the following steps at a high level,

• Identify the team to perform Red Tagging activity.

• Identify and Red Tag the unnecessary items.

• Optionally move these items to the Red Tag area, which is an area to keep red tagged items temporarily for deciding appropriate action.

• Decide the action to be taken on the Red Tagged items (which can be to dispose the item, or move it to another department, or repair it, or keep as it is) through appropriate approvals and authorization.

• Summarize the activity and item(s) in a Red Tagging Register for future reference, capturing relevant details.

The following figure depicts the Red Tagging process at a high level.

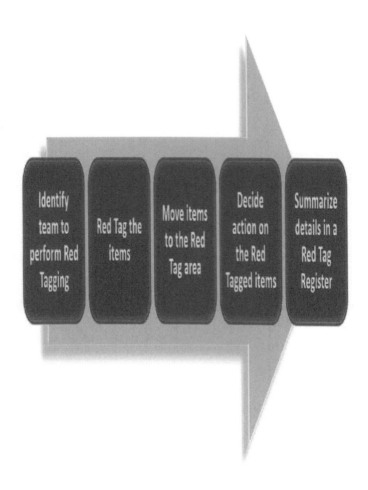

LAYOUT OPTIMIZATION

Layout Optimization is the most effective strategy to keep the workplace in appropriate order, and hence it helps achieve **Seiton** in the workplace.

It is used to check all the items in the workplace, and arrange them in an optimal way for fulfilling their function.

Layout Optimization involves analyzing the work place or area and deciding the best way of arranging items in a logical order, for easy retrieval and selection.

Spaghetti Diagrams which make use of lines that appear like noodles, are the visual representations of the flow of items or data through systems or processes, and are often times used while analyzing the workplace layouts.

The following figure depicts a sample Spaghetti Diagram of Before and After layouts of a sandwich joint, for better understanding.

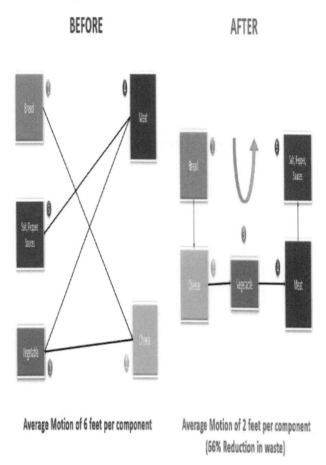

Layout Optimization: Process

Layout Optimization often times involve the following steps at a high level,

• Identify the team to perform layout optimization.

• Map the Spaghetti Diagram capturing the waste of motion/ transport in the current layout.

• Brainstorm and identify ways to improve the arrangement of layout to achieve reduction in wastes of motion and/or transport.

• Map the Spaghetti Diagram to capture the possible motion/transport in the new improved brainstormed layout.

• Present the Before and After Spaghetti Diagrams to the management for approval.

• Implement the new layout post management consent.

• Summarize the improvement details.

Note: Often times, you can even use value stream mapping exercises instead of Spaghetti diagrams.

The following figure depicts the Layout Optimization process at a high level.

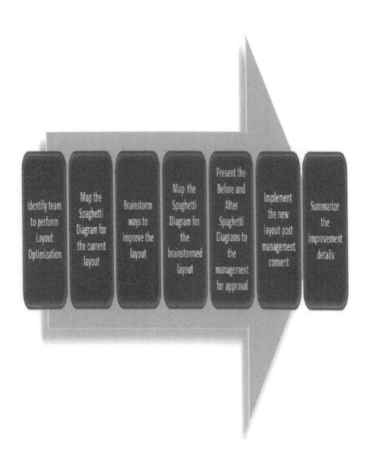

CLEANING SCHEDULE: 5 W AND 1 H

Scheduling Cleaning using the 5W and 1H is the most effective strategy to keep the workplace clean, and hence it helps achieve **Seiso** in the workplace.

It is used to schedule the cleaning and inspecting activities in the workplace, for all the tools, equipment, machinery, and everything else in the it for keeping everything neat and shining.

Scheduling Cleaning using the 5W and 1H involves defining the What, Where, When, Why, Who, and How of the cleaning process, and is used as a proactive mechanism to keep the workplace clean, and shining.

Scheduling Cleaning: 5 W and 1 H

Scheduling Cleaning using 5 W and 1 H most often involves defining the following,

• **What** lists the items that need cleaning and it is a good idea to include all the workplace items.

• **Where** defines the exact location of the items and can be the location where the items reside.

• **When** defines the frequency of cleaning the items and can be based on the how often the items are used.

• **Why** defines the reason for cleaning the items, along with any effects of not cleaning them.

• **Who** defines the people who perform the cleaning, and can be split into accountable and responsible person(s).

• **How** defines the method of cleaning the items, along with the tools used for cleaning them.

The following figure depicts scheduling the cleaning using 5W and 1H for better understanding.

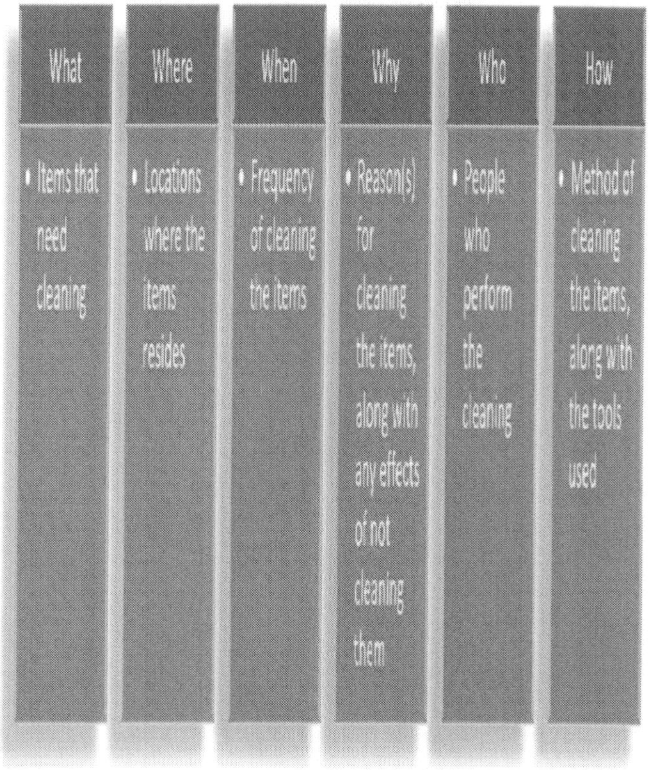

What	Where	When	Why	Who	How
• Items that need cleaning	• Locations where the items resides	• Frequency of cleaning the items	• Reason(s) for cleaning the items, along with any effects of not cleaning them	• People who perform the cleaning	• Method of cleaning the items, along with the tools used

STANDARDIZATION

Standardization is the most effective strategy to establish proper processes, and schedules to perform, and measures to evaluate the first 3S in the workplace, and hence it helps achieve **Seiketsu** in the workplace.

Now we will see how we can develop meaningful standards for the first 3S.

Standards for Seiri Red Tagging

• Develop standard red tag format, for capturing relevant details.

• Identify Red Tag Area and demarcate it with standard color coding.

• Make it mandatory to keep the red tagged items in the identified Red Tag Area.

• Develop a standard format for Red Tag Register, for documenting relevant summary of the Red Tag activity.

Standards for Seiton Layout Optimization

• Develop standards for layout demarcation.

• Develop standard labels, in terms of font, color, for layout optimization.

• Develop standard color coding for layout and location demarcation.

• Develop standard dimensions for items used in the workplace.

• Develop standard specifications for items used in the workplace.

• Develop standards for walkway demarcation in terms of color, width, and other relevant formats.

Standards for Seiso Cleaning Scheduling using 5W and 1H

• Develop standards cleaning schedule format.

• Develop standards to follow the schedule as identified.

• Identify abnormalities that need to be inspected during cleaning process.

• Develop standard action plans to take care of the abnormalities in the workplace.

• Develop standard checklists for cleaning process.

SUSTENANCE FOR SHITSUKE

Some of the best strategies for **Sustaining** the 5S, and hence achieving **Shitsuke** in the workplace are,

• Celebrating 5S days at a regular frequency and interval.

• Awarding best 5S initiatives in terms of rewards and recognition.

• Visual banners, boards, and displays promoting 5S, in the form of quotes, slogans, and essays.

• Presentations and announcements from leadership at regular frequency.

• Newsletters or magazines at regular frequency, containing news and articles on 5S.

• 5S structure for effective implementation of 5S, in terms of dedicated roles, teams, and departments.

- Promoting 5S awareness in form of regular trainings.

- Leadership involvement, support, and focus.

- Regular 5S audits.

Audits

Auditing is the most effective strategy for ensuring ongoing and sustained 5S improvements in the workplace, and hence it helps in achieving **Shitsuke** in the workplace.

Audits are systematic continuous improvement checks that help to determine if the 5S initiative and plans are complied with, and help collect facts and pass them to management for improvement actions.

Audit Cycle begin with **Audit Planning** that involves identifying the work areas to audit, auditors who will perform the audit, schedule to perform the audit, and the audit criteria.

Audit Criteria gives the details on the criteria or the requirements that gives a general idea on performing audits.

Audit Checklists are framed based on the Audit Criteria to identify the points to audit.

Conducting Audit involves checking for **Nonconformance**, which are deviations from the planned 5S initiatives and activities.

Audit Reporting involves summarizing the facts observed during the audit and framing improvement actions to fix the non conformance, along with time line for implementing the actions.

Re-Audits is the last step of the audit cycle and focuses on auditing if the planned action items are implemented.

MANAGEMENT COMMITMENT

Management Commitment is the most important thing needed to keep up the drive and focus on any workplace initiative including the 5S.

It should not happen that the workplace starts the 5S initiative with much interest and once they reach a level of improvement, start neglecting it and losing focus.

Management should continuously focus on keeping up the rigor and drive in the 5S initiative.

Management should provide the necessary resources, time, and support needed to keep up the initiative.

They should encourage and motivate the workforce to participate and contribute.

And most importantly, they should act as role models for the entire workforce, and lead them by example.

AUTHOR'S NOTE

I thank you for choosing the book, I have presented to you a detailed 5S methodology and ways to execute, and implement the 5S process using the most relevant, and effective strategies.

I hope this adds value to you and helps you eliminate wastes, and achieve cost reductions in your processes.

Please leave a review wherever you bought the book, and it will help me in my quest to provide good useful products to you on Lean Six Sigma.

All the very best,

Sumeet Savant
Lean Six Sigma Master Black Belt and Coach

Printed in Great Britain
by Amazon

67598293R00071